YOUNG SAILOR

SHERIDAN HOUSE

Developed by Mark A. Bashforth

Designed by Bob Mathias

Edited by Basil Mosenthal

Text by Andrew Langley

Illustrated by
Robin Lawrie and Bob Mathias

Published 1993 by Sheridan House
145 Palisade Street, Dobbs Ferry, NY 10522

Copyright © 1993 International Log Book A/S

Library of Congress Cataloging-in-Publication Data

Young sailor/ [edited by Basil Mosenthal ; text by Andrew Langley ;
    illustrated by Robin Lawrie and Bob Mathias]
      p.   cm.
    Includes index.
    ISBN 0-924486-61-9
      1. Boating for children--Juvenile literature.   I. Mosenthal,
Basil. II. Langley, Andrew. III. Lawrie, Robin. IV. Mathias, Bob.
GV777.56.Y68   1993
796.1--dc20   93-14201
                                                                CIP
                                                                AC
Printed and bound in Singapore

CONTENTS

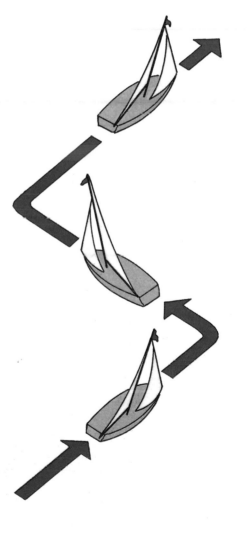

There are many ways to begin sailing. You do not
have to start on the sea. Plenty of boating takes
place on rivers, lakes and reservoirs. Wherever you
live, you won't be far from water.
Nor do you need your own boat. You can rent a
sailboard or use a boat belonging to a club or sailing
school. Or go sailing with an experienced friend.
You may be lucky enough to be offered a boat of
your own. Even so it is better to wait until you have
some sailing experience. Then you will know what
kind of boat suits you best.

Learning the Basics

Learning to windsurf or to sail a simple
dinghy is not difficult. You will very soon be
able to get afloat on your own.

You can learn a lot by crewing for others. Some
dinghies need a crew of two or three, and any
helmsman is glad to have a good partner. You can
get just as much pleasure from crewing as you can
from being at the helm – especially during races.
▼

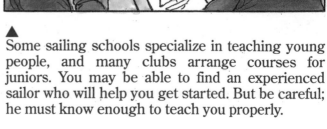

▲
Some sailing schools specialize in teaching young
people, and many clubs arrange courses for
juniors. You may be able to find an experienced
sailor who will help you get started. But be careful;
he must know enough to teach you properly.

Windsurfing is a great way to start sailing. Many people find it so exciting that they prefer sailboards to larger boats.

Racing

Many clubs organize dinghy racing for juniors. This is great fun, and a good way of learning to sail well.

To win races you must know how to get the best out of your boat and make it go faster than the others.

But you will also need to learn and understand the racing rules. And if you are racing near the sea you must certainly know about the local tides.

A group of '420s' enjoy a brisk afternoon's club racing.

Many classes of sailing dinghy are suitable for a beginner. Visit your local sailing area and you will see the most popular types available. This will help you decide which boat is best for you.

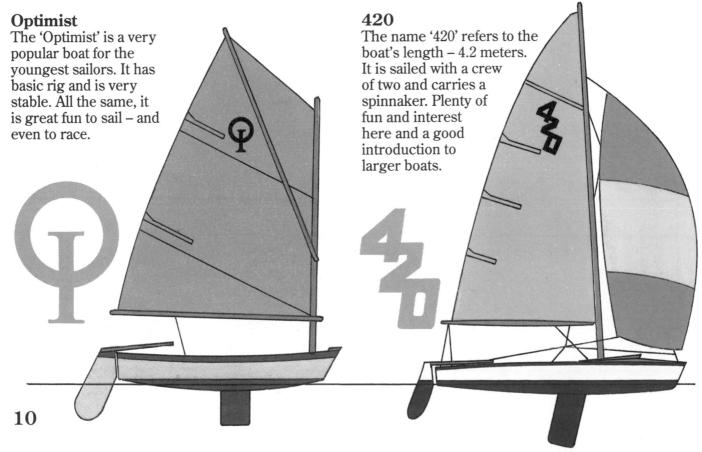

Optimist

The 'Optimist' is a very popular boat for the youngest sailors. It has basic rig and is very stable. All the same, it is great fun to sail – and even to race.

420

The name '420' refers to the boat's length – 4.2 meters. It is sailed with a crew of two and carries a spinnaker. Plenty of fun and interest here and a good introduction to larger boats.

A dinghy can be powered by an outboard motor or with oars, but it should always carry oars as well in case the motor breaks down or runs out of fuel. Every sailor must know how to use a pair of oars. This is one of the basic skills of seamanship.

Inflatable dinghies are ▶ very popular. They are often carried by yachts and used as tenders to take the crew ashore when at anchor.

Laser
The 'Laser' is a very fast boat, much used for racing. But its rig is simple and with some experience young sailors can enjoy this exciting boat.

Sailboard
Sailboards are light enough for one person to carry, and will fit on a car roof rack. They can be launched from a beach or the shore of a lake, which means you can windsurf almost anywhere.

SEA TERMS

Sailors may sometimes seem to have a language of their own. There are so many things that are special to ships and the sea, that there must be special terms to describe them. If you are going to be around boats – to rig them, to sail them, to talk about them with your friends – then you must learn the correct terms.

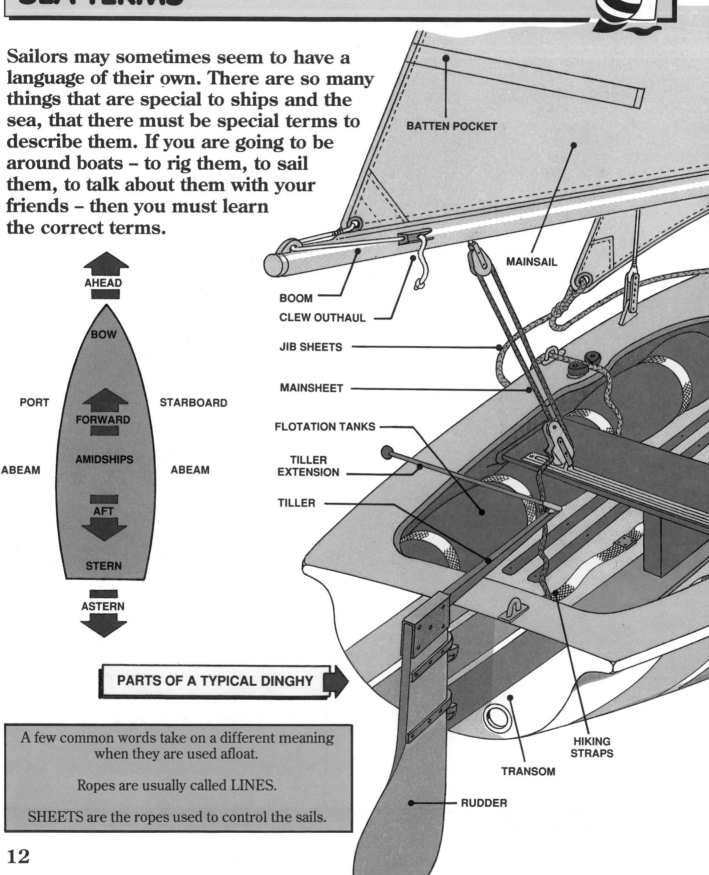

AHEAD

BOW

PORT   STARBOARD

FORWARD

ABEAM   AMIDSHIPS   ABEAM

AFT

STERN

ASTERN

BATTEN POCKET

MAINSAIL

BOOM

CLEW OUTHAUL

JIB SHEETS

MAINSHEET

FLOTATION TANKS

TILLER EXTENSION

TILLER

HIKING STRAPS

TRANSOM

RUDDER

PARTS OF A TYPICAL DINGHY

A few common words take on a different meaning when they are used afloat.

Ropes are usually called LINES.

SHEETS are the ropes used to control the sails.

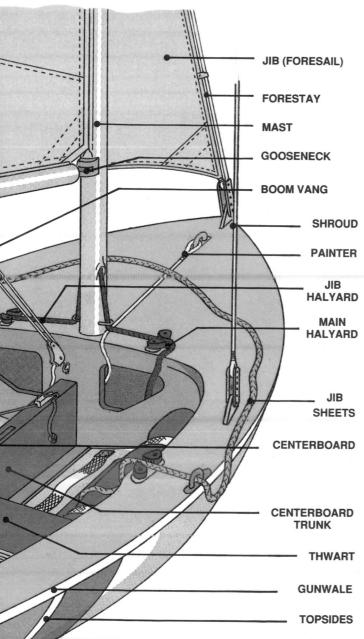

JIB (FORESAIL)

FORESTAY

MAST

GOOSENECK

BOOM VANG

SHROUD

PAINTER

JIB HALYARD

MAIN HALYARD

JIB SHEETS

CENTERBOARD

CENTERBOARD TRUNK

THWART

GUNWALE

TOPSIDES

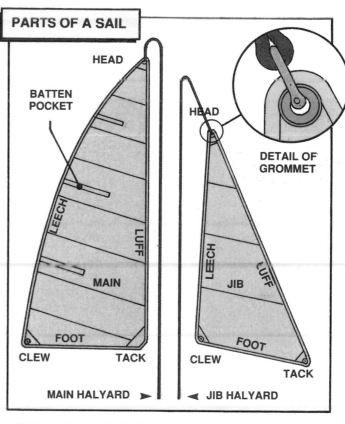

PARTS OF A SAIL

HEAD

BATTEN POCKET

LEECH

LUFF

MAIN

FOOT

CLEW   TACK

HEAD

DETAIL OF GROMMET

LEECH

LUFF

JIB

FOOT

CLEW   TACK

MAIN HALYARD ▶   ◀ JIB HALYARD

Halyards and rigging

Halyard – the line used to hoist a sail.
Thus main halyard and jib halyard.
Sheet – the line used to control a sail.
Thus main sheet and jib sheet.
Mainsail – clearly the name for the main sail.
Jib – the smaller sail forward of the mast.
Rigging – the wires supporting the mast.
Forestay – the wire from the masthead to the bow.
Shrouds – supporting wires on either side of the mast.

CENTERBOARD

A *centerboard* is a plate, usually hinged at the top front corner, which can be raised or lowered as necessary.

DAGGERBOARD

A *daggerboard,* usually made of wood and not secured to the boat. It can be raised or lowered (like a dagger in a sheath).

FIXED KEEL

A *fixed keel* is part of the structure of the hull. Obviously it cannot be altered.

Here are some of the many fittings (and pieces of hardware) found in any boat. They may be used in a super-tanker just as well as in a sailing dinghy. It is a matter of size!

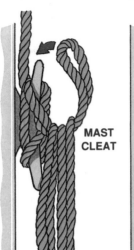

MAST CLEAT

◄**Cleats**
Cleats are used for securing lines such as the halyards on a sailing boat.

You may also see cleats on a ► dock for securing mooring lines.

MOORING CLEAT

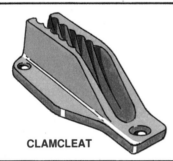

CLAMCLEAT

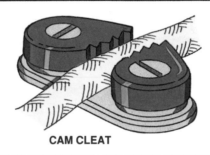

CAM CLEAT

◄ Jam cleats are often used in racing boats. The line is held firmly, but it can be released quickly. As you can see, they operate with a cam action.

Shackles
These are used in many places and come in many sizes. For instance to secure the main sheet to the boom and the main halyard to the head of the mainsail.

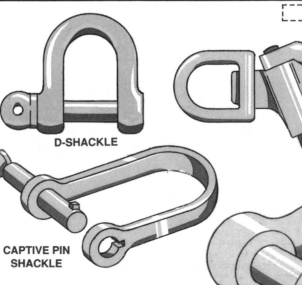

D-SHACKLE

SWIVEL SNAP-SHACKLE

BOW SHACKLE

CAPTIVE PIN SHACKLE

LARGE ANCHOR SHACKLE

Anchors

There are various types of anchors although they are all designed to do the same thing – to dig into the mud or sand and hold the boat.

'Plow' anchors, which are used by many yachts, are designed on the principle of a plow share, which digs into the earth.

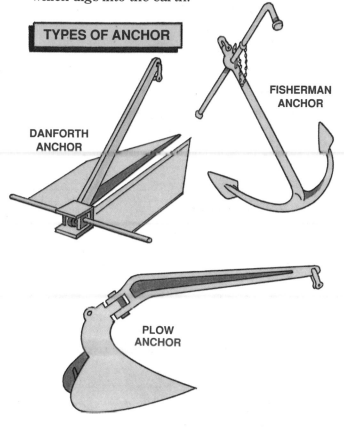

TYPES OF ANCHOR

DANFORTH ANCHOR

FISHERMAN ANCHOR

PLOW ANCHOR

Shackle Keys and Marlinspikes

Shackle pins may be undone with a spike, or with a *shackle key.* You must be careful not to loose shackle pins, but many are made so that they cannot drop out of the shackle. *Marlinspikes* are also used for splicing.

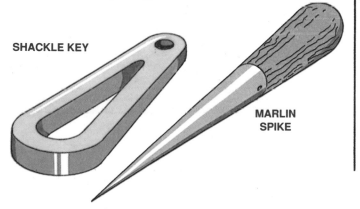

SHACKLE KEY

MARLIN SPIKE

Blocks

A *block* is like a pulley. Modern blocks used in yachts and dinghies are made of steel and plastic, with a *sheave* which rotates. You will see single, double, or even larger blocks.

Blocks were originally made from wood, and these are still used, especially in larger yachts.

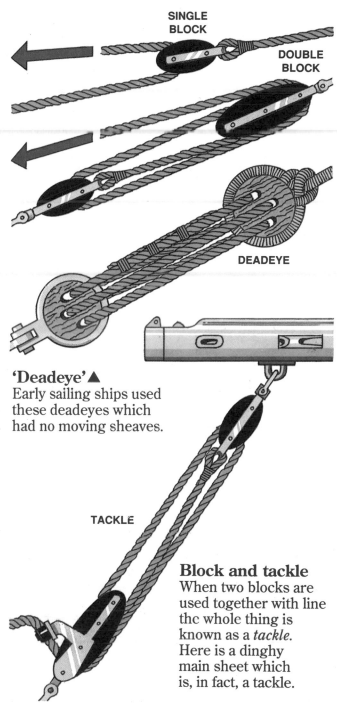

SINGLE BLOCK

DOUBLE BLOCK

DEADEYE

'Deadeye' ▲
Early sailing ships used these deadeyes which had no moving sheaves.

TACKLE

Block and tackle
When two blocks are used together with line the whole thing is known as a *tackle.* Here is a dinghy main sheet which is, in fact, a tackle.

LOOKING AFTER YOUR BOAT

Any type of boat, whether it is a sailboard or a dinghy, needs looking after properly. This applies just as much to a borrowed boat as to one you own.

Before you go sailing you must learn how to rig your boat. And you will soon find that your rig has a lot of small parts. If any of these are lost or broken, they will be expensive to replace. What's more, the boat is out of action for a time.

When you unrig a boat, make sure that all the gear is kept together and stowed away properly.

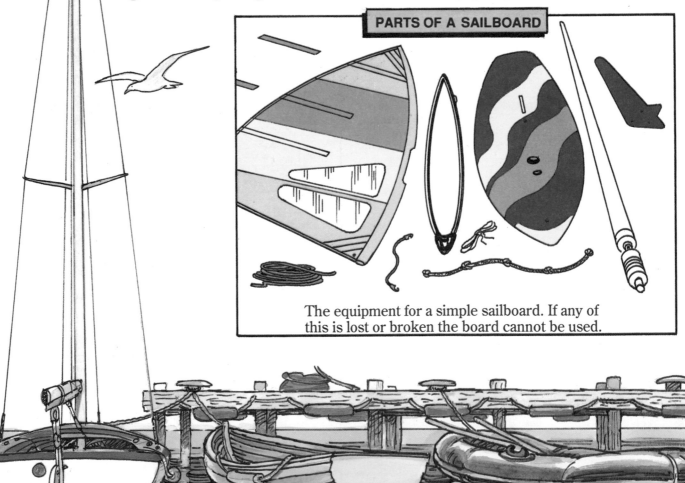

PARTS OF A SAILBOARD

The equipment for a simple sailboard. If any of this is lost or broken the board cannot be used.

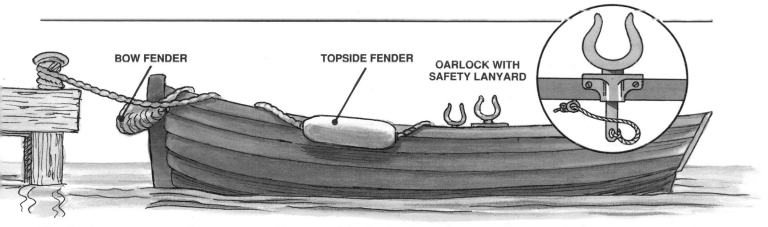

BOW FENDER   TOPSIDE FENDER   OARLOCK WITH SAFETY LANYARD

Use fenders to prevent damage when securing your dinghy alongside another boat or when tied to a dock.

Always pull in the fenders when you are underway. It looks sloppy and unseamanlike to leave them hanging over the side.

Some oarlocks are permanently fitted. If not, they must always have lanyards attached so that they will not be lost overboard.

Using a boat with an engine
Before taking out a boat with an engine always check that there is enough fuel. Also make sure that you have oars and oarlocks.

Some engines can be difficult to start. There is usually a special way of using the throttle and the choke. Make sure you know it.

This outboard motor has a safety lanyard which is secured to the boat in case the regular mounting fails. The lanyard may also be used for safety when passing the engine into the boat. Many outboard motors are lost overboard.

▼

What a boat should carry
- Adequate bow and stern painters
- Oars and oarlocks even with an outboard engine
- A plastic bailer, secured to the boat with a lanyard (a bailer may be made by cutting down a large plastic container)
- A sponge for wiping up small amounts of water is useful
- At night or in fog, a flashlight is a must.

At sea, a boat sailing far from its base will usually carry a small anchor and line.

When you have finished using a boat
When leaving a boat remove the oars from the oarlocks (unless they are fixed), or they may get broken or lost. The oarlocks on the inflatable *(left)* are fixed and cannot be removed. There is no need to use fenders with an inflatable, but the fabric must still be treated with care.

As well as leaving the boat neat, and the gear stowed tidily, always leave it dry. If the boat is hauled ashore, it can be emptied by removing the drainplugs. Make sure they are replaced, and always check the plugs before launching a boat.

SAILING YOUR DINGHY

You can only learn to sail by practicing in a boat or on a sailboard. Your first steps will be much easier if you understand some of the basic principles of sailing – and some of the terms. The first thing to understand is that you cannot sail directly into the wind. You can only sail to within about 45 degrees of the wind direction; some boats can sail closer to the wind than others.

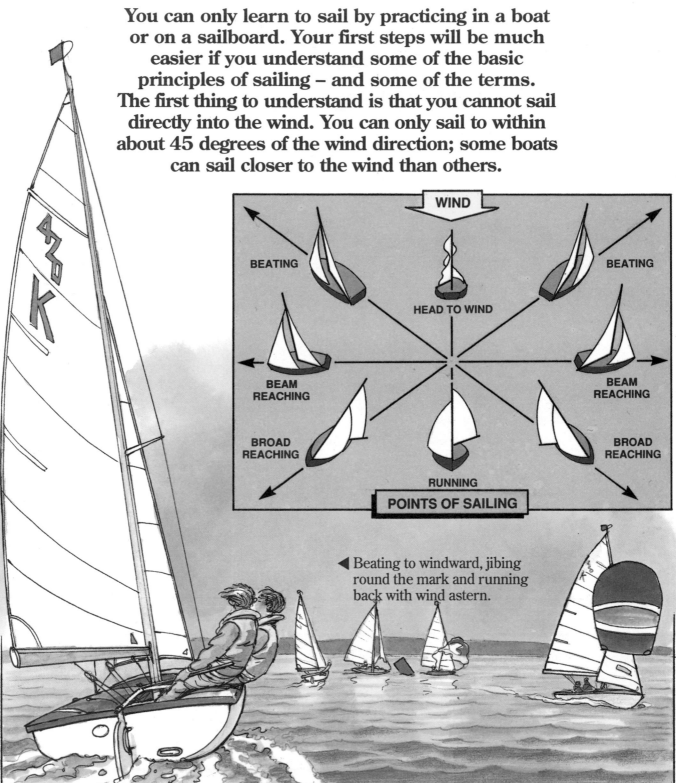

WIND

BEATING

BEATING

HEAD TO WIND

BEAM REACHING

BEAM REACHING

BROAD REACHING

BROAD REACHING

RUNNING

POINTS OF SAILING

◀ Beating to windward, jibing round the mark and running back with wind astern.

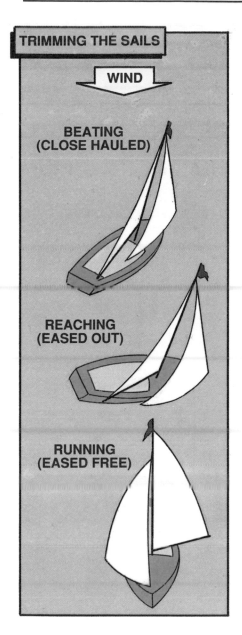

TRIMMING THE SAILS

WIND

BEATING (CLOSE HAULED)

REACHING (EASED OUT)

RUNNING (EASED FREE)

The sails

When you are beating to windward your sails are *close hauled.* That means the sheets are hauled in.

When you are *reaching* the sheets are eased out. They are eased out further when you are *running free.*

These rules are the same whether you have only a mainsail or a mainsail and a jib.

Tacking

If you want to steer towards the wind *(beating to windward)*, you have to steer a zig-zag course. When you turn through the wind you are *tacking* or *coming about,* putting the wind on the opposite side of the boat.

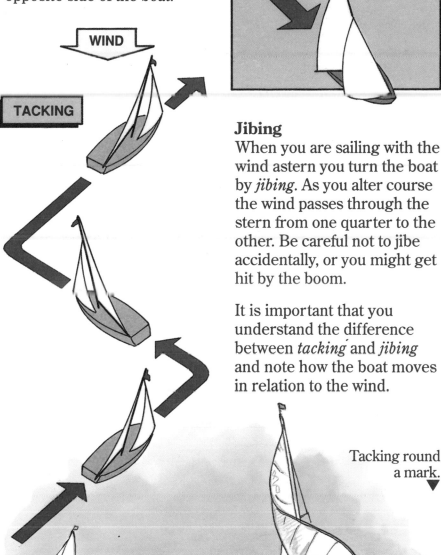

WIND

TACKING

JIBING

WIND

Jibing

When you are sailing with the wind astern you turn the boat by *jibing.* As you alter course the wind passes through the stern from one quarter to the other. Be careful not to jibe accidentally, or you might get hit by the boom.

It is important that you understand the difference between *tacking* and *jibing* and note how the boat moves in relation to the wind.

Tacking round a mark.
▼

WINDSURFING

The principles of sailing are the same for any craft. But a windsurfer is rigged and handled in quite a different way from a dinghy. Before you start, you must know the main parts of your sailboard, and how to rig it. The foot of the mast fits into a universal joint so that the mast can swivel in any direction. The wishbone acts as a boom to hold out the sail, but you also hold onto it and use it to control the rig. The clear plastic sail window lets you see where you are going.

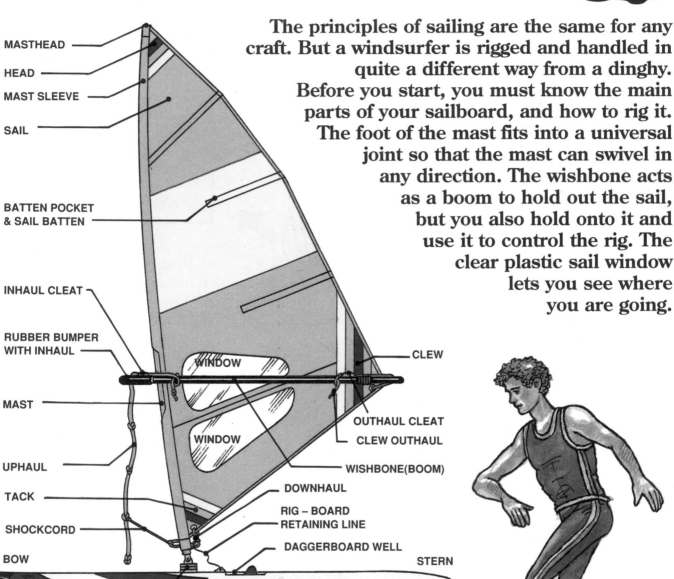

MASTHEAD

HEAD

MAST SLEEVE

SAIL

BATTEN POCKET & SAIL BATTEN

INHAUL CLEAT

RUBBER BUMPER WITH INHAUL

MAST

UPHAUL

TACK

SHOCKCORD

BOW

WINDOW

WINDOW

CLEW

OUTHAUL CLEAT

CLEW OUTHAUL

WISHBONE(BOOM)

DOWNHAUL

RIG – BOARD RETAINING LINE

DAGGERBOARD WELL

STERN

MAST PIVOT & UNIVERSAL JOINT

DAGGERBOARD

SKEG OF FIN

PARTS OF A SAILBOARD

Standing and steering
Good balance is very important for windsurfing. You must practice standing up and getting used to moving around the board.

There is no rudder on a sailboard. Instead you learn to steer by tilting the boom up and down.

You use the sail as you would in a dinghy. The points of sail are the same.

▲ To achieve good balance practice standing up on an un-rigged board. Once you have mastered this, you will find a fully rigged board easier to handle.

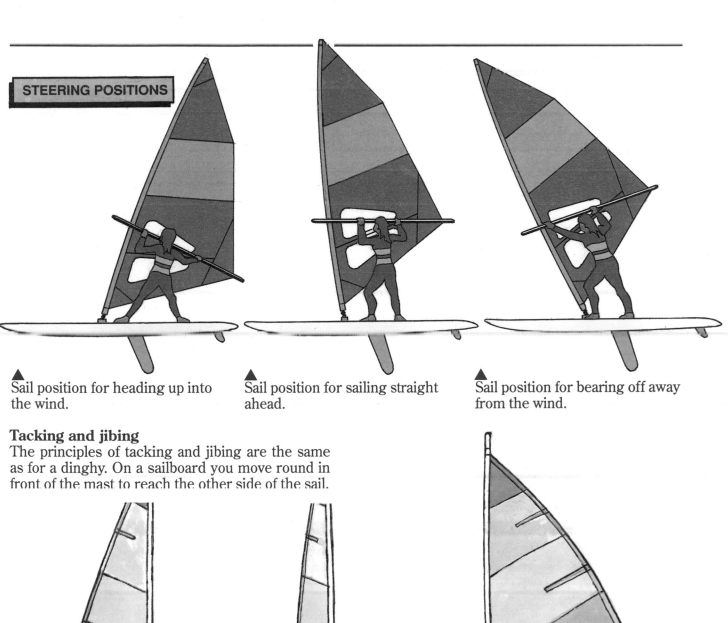

▲ Sail position for heading up into the wind.

▲ Sail position for sailing straight ahead.

▲ Sail position for bearing off away from the wind.

Tacking and jibing
The principles of tacking and jibing are the same as for a dinghy. On a sailboard you move round in front of the mast to reach the other side of the sail.

▲ On starboard tack, moving round the bow and preparing to go about.

▲ Head to the wind with board steady, moving round in front of the mast.

▲ Going through tack and moving aft to begin sailing on port tack.

ROPES AND KNOTS

Sailors have always known how to handle ropes and tie knots. The old sailing ships had masses of sails and complicated rigging. Nowadays things are much simpler, but even rigging a sailboard needs some knots.

Types of Rope

Almost all of today's ropes are made from artificial fiber, which is very strong and durable. You may still see the old-fashioned ropes made from vegetable fiber such as manila and sisal.

Two main types of rope are used aboard ships and yachts.

REGULAR - 3 STRAND LAID ROPE

◀ The regular rope consisting of three strands twisted together.

BRAIDED ROPE

◀ Braid is made by weaving a braid around a center core.

POLYPROPYLENE ROPE

◀ Polypropylene rope is usually brightly colored in orange or yellow. It is used mainly for water skiing because it floats. However it is not as strong as regular rope, and is slippery. Knots tied in polypropylene easily come undone.

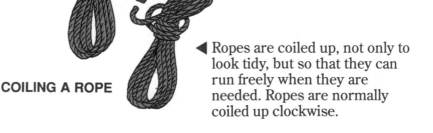

COILING A ROPE

◀ Ropes are coiled up, not only to look tidy, but so that they can run freely when they are needed. Ropes are normally coiled up clockwise.

REEF KNOT

Essentially for tying reefs in sails, but also used for joining two ropes of the *same* size (not ropes of different sizes; it may slip)

FIGURE OF EIGHT KNOT

Known as a 'stopper knot'. Usually tied to prevent a rope from running out through a block, for instance in the ends of sheets.

ROUND TURN AND TWO HALF HITCHES

A basic knot used for tying a line around a bar or a post. Note that the phrase 'round turn' means that there are really two turns.

BOWLINE

For tying an eye at the end of a rope. May need practice at first. Easy to untie, but it cannot slip if it is tied properly.

SHEET BEND

For joining two ropes of different sizes. Becomes a Double Sheet Bend when passed around twice.

CLOVE HITCH

For securing a line to a rail or ring.

For securing a rope to a rail or to another rope. Useful because it will hold with a sideways pull, and is much better than a Clove Hitch in this instance.

Knots and their uses

There are two things to remember about knots:

- Each has a special purpose, and there is always a proper knot for the job being done
- A proper knot will never work loose on its own, but is easy to untie when needed

Here are seven knots which are commonly used afloat and which every sailor should be able to tie.

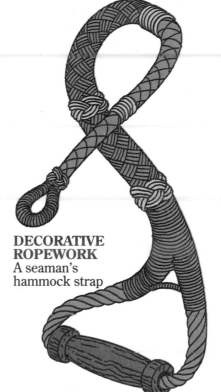

DECORATIVE ROPEWORK
A seaman's hammock strap

Ropes' ends

An untidy rope's end is always said to be the sign of a careless sailor. If neglected too long the rope will become useless.

A whipping is the neatest and most secure way of fixing the end of a line. The best job is done with waxed thread known as *whipping twine*

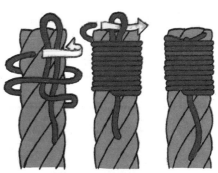

COMMON WHIPPING

WATCHING THE WEATHER

The weather has always played an important part in a sailor's life. Before the days of steam and diesel engines, sailing ships depended completely on the wind and weather. Anyone who sails a yacht or small boat today must still be concerned with the weather. It makes all the difference to their enjoyment – and their safety.

Weather Forecasts

Unlike the early sailors, we have weather forecasts. We can get them from the newspapers, by phone, or on television. Some areas even have a weather channel, which has forecasts for sailors.

But why listen to a forecast when you can see for yourself what the weather is like? For a start some idea about the future weather will help you plan ahead.

Suppose the weather looks good in the morning, but last night's forecast promised storms. You would still go sailing, but you wouldn't go far, and you would watch carefully for signs of change.

▲
In fine weather, with a gentle breeze blowing (not above force 3 – see page 28), the sea conditions are pleasant with low waves and ideal for exciting sailing.

▲
If the wind strength increases (force 5-6), even though the sun still shines, the sea can become rough with large waves making it unsuitable for sailing small craft.

Local Weather

You may find that the weather in your local area is different from the main forecast. This is because general forecasts cover a large area, and the weather does not always obey the rules. Weather fronts may move faster or slower than expected or change direction altogether.

Check your local forecast at your marina or clubhouse before you put to sea.

WATCH THE CLOUDS

FAIR WEATHER CLOUDS

BE CAREFUL!
COULD BE BAD WEATHER

◀ **Keeping a Weather Eye**
The weather can change swiftly and unexpectedly. So, even though you know the official forecast, you must always keep a careful watch while you are sailing. Approaching clouds are the most usual warning of bad weather, and a shift in the wind direction can also mean change.

If you want to understand weather forecasts properly, you should learn to read a weather map. These are shown in TV weather forecasts and in the newspapers. On TV you see various maps: some show the weather conditions and some show the weather systems that create the weather.

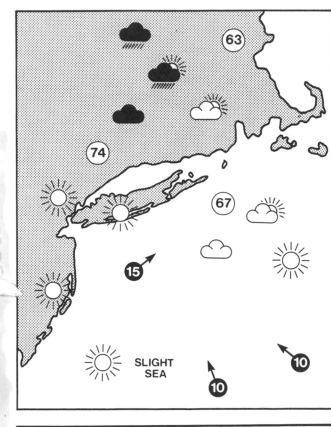

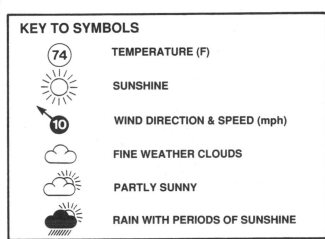

KEY TO SYMBOLS

- 74   **TEMPERATURE (F)**
- **SUNSHINE**
- 10   **WIND DIRECTION & SPEED (mph)**
- **FINE WEATHER CLOUDS**
- **PARTLY SUNNY**
- **RAIN WITH PERIODS OF SUNSHINE**

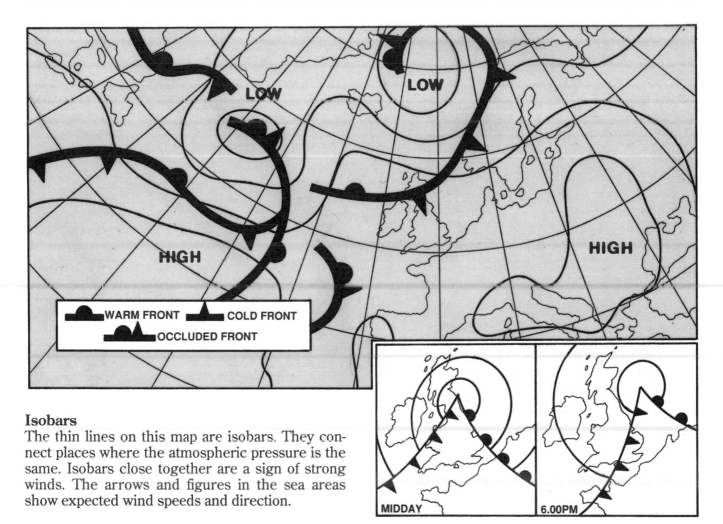

WARM FRONT   **COLD FRONT**
OCCLUDED FRONT

MIDDAY   **6.00PM**

Isobars
The thin lines on this map are isobars. They connect places where the atmospheric pressure is the same. Isobars close together are a sign of strong winds. The arrows and figures in the sea areas show expected wind speeds and direction.

Highs and Lows
These are areas of high or low barometric pressure. Where there is high pressure the weather will generally be fine and calm, though in winter this can also mean fog and frost. Low pressure almost always produces bad weather.

Fronts
Fronts are areas of warm or cold air on the move, and usually bring a period of unsettled weather. Cold fronts cause worse weather than warm ones and travel faster, gradually overtaking the warm front. This results in an occluded front.

This 'low', with the isobars close ▶ together, indicates a severe gale. The arrows on the isobars show the wind direction. You can see that the wind blows counter clockwise around it (in the Northern hemisphere). It will blow clockwise around a 'high'. From this you should be able to work out how the wind will change as a 'high' or 'low' passes over.

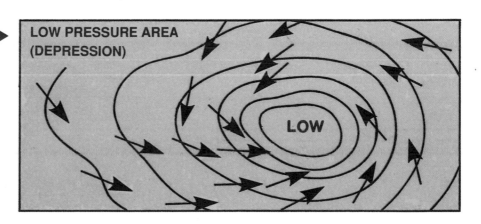

LOW PRESSURE AREA (DEPRESSION)

LOW

THE WIND

The wind affects sailors more than anything else. If there is no wind and a hot sun it is fine for sunbathing, but not for sailing. Too much wind will bring rough seas, and you will not be able to sail at all.

Wind Speed

On weather maps wind speed is usually shown in miles per hour. But there are two other ways in which sailors refer to wind speed – in knots, and by means of the Beaufort Scale. This was devised in 1806 by Admiral Sir Francis Beaufort, and is now in use throughout the world.

A knot is one nautical mile per hour, and a nautical mile is 2000 yards (1852 meters).

You have probably already heard the Beaufort Scale being used – for instance by reference to 'Gale force 8' in a radio gale warning or Small Craft Advisory.

THE BEAUFORT SCALE			
Force	**Speed (knots)**	**Description**	
0	0-1	Calm	
1	1-3	Light air	
2	4-6	Light breeze	
3	7-10	Gentle breeze	
4	11-16	Moderate breeze	
5	17-21	Fresh breeze	
6	22-27	Strong breeze	
7	28-33	Near gale	
8	34-40	Gale	
9	41-47	Severe gale	Not the weather for us to be sailing
10	48-55	Storm	
11	56-63	Violent storm	
12	64 plus	Hurricane	

Judging the Wind

With a little experience you will be able to look at the weather and decide if the wind is suitable for sailing.

But how do you relate what you see to an actual wind strength? The forecast may say that the winds will be Force 4. How do you know if this will suit you? The pictures (opposite) give some indication of how the sea is with various wind strengths.

Descriptions of wind strength are deceptive. A 'breeze' may sound gentle, but a 'fresh breeze' of Force 5 will be too much for most small craft. Beginners with dinghies or sailboards will do very nicely with winds of Force 2 – 3.

The effects of the wind may be felt less on inland waters. There will be no big waves – although it is just as easy to capsize on a river as in the sea!

Offshore Winds

It is especially hard to judge the strength of the wind when it is blowing offshore (from the shore towards the sea). An offshore breeze often feels lighter on the beach than out at sea.

▲

The wind also feels lighter when your boat is running with it. You must always take care when you are running before an offshore breeze. When you turn into the wind to head back to shore you may find it harder than you expected.

The Big Winds

Anyone who has been in a gale knows that it is uncomfortable and often frightening, especially in a small yacht. Winds can be over 40 knots and seas up to 20ft.

Winds of over 70 knots are not uncommon in a bad winter. This can mean 40ft waves. Remember that the Coast Guard is often called to the rescue in that sort of weather!

In hurricanes, typhoons, and other tropical storms, gusts of well over 100 knots are common. If you have never experienced them, it is hard to imagine such strong winds.

It is usually easy to see if the sea is at high tide or low tide, (sailors talk of 'high water and low water'). In most places, low water comes about 6¼ hours after high water. Although you can work out the times of high and low water roughly, seamen use Tide Tables. These give the exact times and heights for each area along the coast.

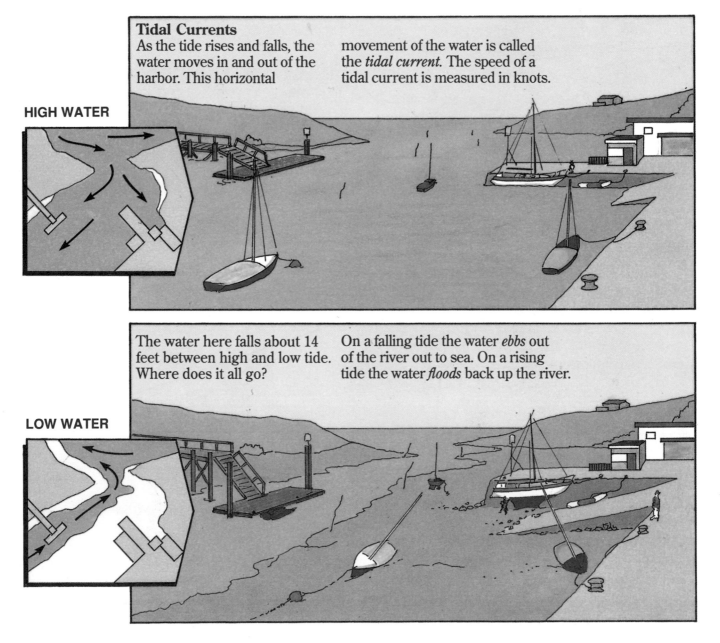

Tidal Currents
As the tide rises and falls, the water moves in and out of the harbor. This horizontal movement of the water is called the *tidal current*. The speed of a tidal current is measured in knots.

HIGH WATER

The water here falls about 14 feet between high and low tide. Where does it all go?

On a falling tide the water *ebbs* out of the river out to sea. On a rising tide the water *floods* back up the river.

LOW WATER

Tidal range

The amount that a tide rises and falls is called its *tidal range*. This varies in different places depending on the distance from the equator. For example, there is almost no tide in the Caribbean sea.

Some of the highest tides in the world occur in the Bay of Fundy in Nova Scotia. The range there is as much as 44 feet.

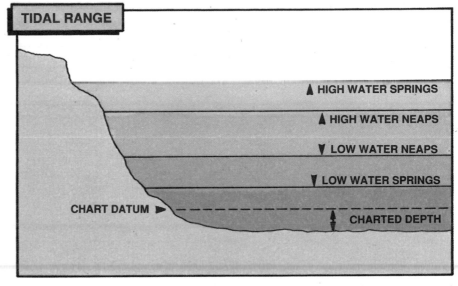

TIDAL RANGE

▲ HIGH WATER SPRINGS
▲ HIGH WATER NEAPS
▼ LOW WATER NEAPS
▼ LOW WATER SPRINGS
CHART DATUM ▶
CHARTED DEPTH

Slack Water

The tide does not simply flood in, jam on the brakes, and ebb out again. As high water approaches the tidal current slows down, and hardly moves. This is called 'slack water'. There is another period of slack water at low tide.

When you sail across ▶ the tidal current, you must make allowance for it. The progress of this dinghy is different from the course being steered.

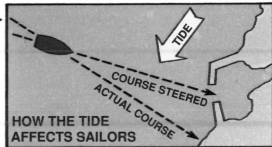

TIDE

COURSE STEERED

ACTUAL COURSE

HOW THE TIDE AFFECTS SAILORS

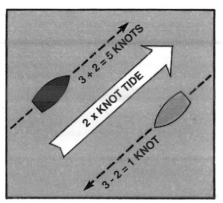

3 + 2 = 5 KNOTS

2 x KNOT TIDE

3 - 2 = 1 KNOT

◀ If you are sailing against the tide at 3 knots, you seem to be moving fast but you are making little progress. But if you are sailing with the tide at 3 knots you are sailing much faster than appears.

ALWAYS KNOW WHAT THE TIDE IS DOING

3 HOURS AFTER HIGH WATER

SANDBANK!

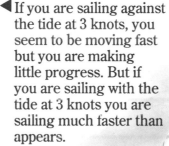

HIGH WATER

SANDBANK

Local knowledge

Wherever they sail, good sailors always know what the tide is doing, and where it is strongest. For instance, in a river the tide often flows more strongly in the middle than it does at the sides. There may even be an eddy close inshore flowing in a different direction.

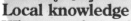

31

Finding your way on inland waters is rarely a problem. But at sea you will need help to know where you are. Nautical charts are the road maps of the sea.

There are many kinds of charts. Some cover whole oceans, while others show only a length of coastline or a harbor entrance.

Charts of American waters are published by NOAA, an agency of the U.S. Department of Commerce.

Here are two sections of charts to show you what they look like. The large chart opposite showing the area round Land's End is the type a vessel would use when sailing along the coast. The large scale chart of Penzance harbor would be used for sailing into the harbor.

Charts use many symbols and abbreviations; some of the less obvious are explained opposite. Various colours are used on charts. Here the sea is white, although shallow water is shown in blue. The area shown in green is only visible at low water. The small purple blips indicate lighthouses and lighted buoys.

Charts also show features on the land, particularly those that are easily seen and identified from the sea.

Soundings
A chart tells you not only what you can see, but what you can't see! Look out across a harbor. You can't tell how deep the water is. But the chart and the Tide Tables will tell you.

The figures dotted over the sea areas show the depths at that point. They are known as *soundings*. Of course the depths will vary as the tide rises and falls. The soundings on a chart always show the *least* depth which can be expected in that spot – the depth at low water springs.

All sailors must know the depth of water if they are to navigate safely. Even a small yacht may have a keel which projects 6 feet below the water (as sailors say, she 'draws' 6 feet) and a dinghy with a center board can easily run aground. A big ship may easily draw 30 feet or more.

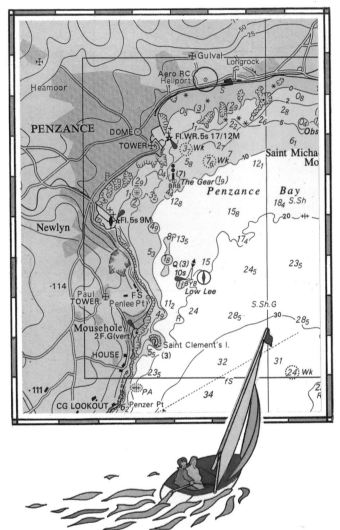

Crown Copyright. Reproduced from Admiralty Chart 777 with the permission of the Controller of Her Majesty's Stationery Office.

See if you can find these details on the big chart.

- There isn't a lighthouse on Land's End, but the Longships Lighthouse is on a rock one mile off-shore. This light has a range of 19 miles and although the main beam is white, there are some sectors where a red light shows.
- Further north, there is a big light on the mainland at Pendeen.
- The Runnel Stone, a dangerous rock off the southernmost point of the coast, is marked by a lighted buoy.
- There is a Coastguard Station at Sennen Cove, which is close to Land's End and slightly to the North.

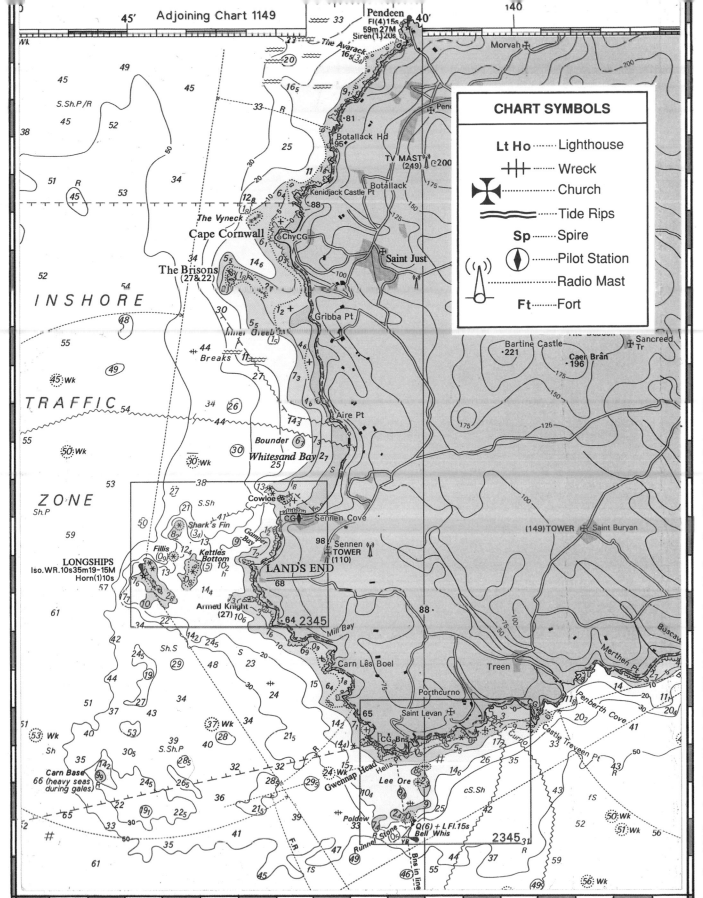

CHART SYMBOLS

Lt Ho	Lighthouse
✝	Wreck
✠	Church
〰〰	Tide Rips
Sp	Spire
⬙	Pilot Station
⋔	Radio Mast
Ft	Fort

Pendeen
Fl(4)15s
59m 27M
Siren(1)20s

The Avarack
16₅

Morvah

Botallack Hd
95

TV MAST
(249)   C200

Botallack

Kenidjack Castle Pt
88

Saint Just

The Vyneck

Cape Cornwall

ChyCG

The Brisons
(27 & 22)

INSHORE

Gribba Pt

Bartine Castle
·221

Caer Brân
·196

Sancreed
Tr

Inner Creeb

Breaks

TRAFFIC

Aire Pt

Wk

Bounder

Whitesand Bay

ZONE
Sh.P

Cowloe

Sennen Cove

(149) TOWER   Saint Buryan

Shark's Fin

Gamper Bay

98 Sennen
TOWER
(110)

Fillis

Kettles Bottom

LONGSHIPS
Iso.WR.10s35m19-15M
Horn(1)10s

LAND'S END

Armed Knight
(27)

Mill Bay

Carn Lês Boel

Treen

Porthcurno

Saint Levan

Penberth Cove

Castle Treryn Pt

Carn Base
66 (heavy seas
during gales)

Gwennap Head

Hella Pt

Lee Ore

cS.Sh

Wk

Poldew

Runnel Stone
Q(6)+L Fl.15s
Bell Whis

Bns in line

2345

Wk

Crown Copyright. Reproduced from Admiralty Chart 777 with the permission of the Controller of Her Majesty's Stationery Office.

Measuring Distance on a Chart

Most large scale and harbor charts have a scale like a road map. The distances are shown in feet and meters. But the sailor's normal way of measuring distance is by using the latitude scale on the side of the chart. One minute of latitude equals one nautical mile (2,000 yards, or 1852 meters).

The drawing *(right)* shows how a pair of dividers is used to measure off the scale.

The dividers are spread between the ▶ two points on the chart. The dividers are then moved to the scale at the side of the chart to measure the distance in nautical miles.

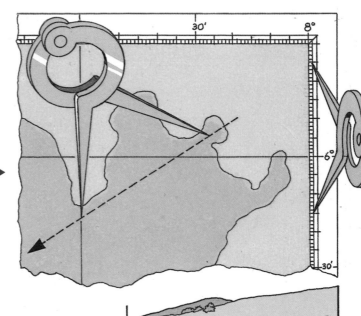

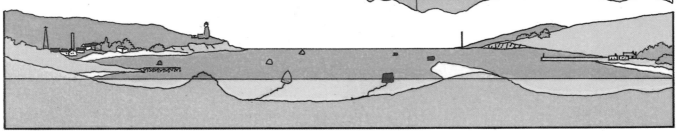

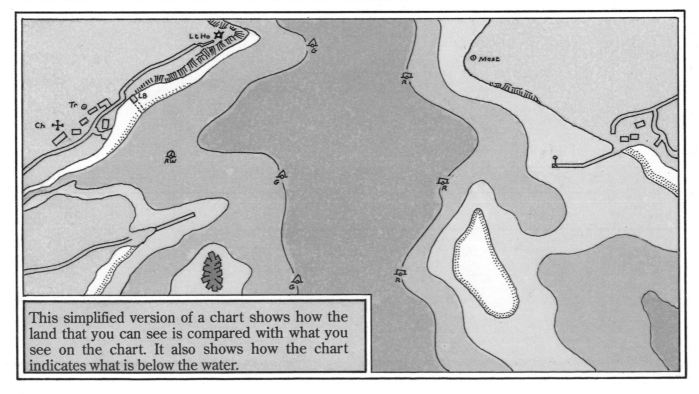

This simplified version of a chart shows how the land that you can see is compared with what you see on the chart. It also shows how the chart indicates what is below the water.

If you want to sail across an estuary, you aim at an object and steer towards it, making an allowance for the tide. But what do you do if there is a thick fog and you cannot see the other side? How do you steer when you are out at sea and can see no land at all?
The answer is by using a compass. Yachts and small craft use magnetic compasses, while big yachts and merchant ships use gyro compasses.

The Compass

A typical mariner's compass fitted in a yacht. The magnets are fixed under the compass card. The card can pivot so that it always stays level. It floats in a liquid which prevents it from moving too violently.

Although figures are now used for compass courses, the Cardinal points are still shown on the compass card. For example, South is 180 degrees.

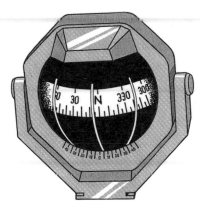

COMPASS

COMPASS CARD

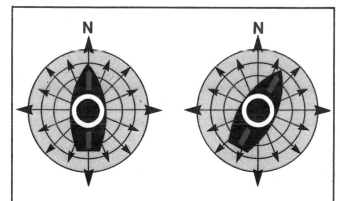

The Lubber's Line

A magnetic compass always points to Magnetic North, which differs from True North depending on where you are on the globe. On a ship's compass the lubber's line always points in the direction the vessel is going. As you change course, the lubber's line moves, but the compass needle remains pointing to the North. With practice it is easy

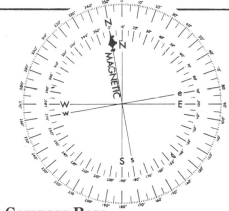

The Compass Rose

This represents the compass card on the chart. The difference between the two circles is the difference between True North and Magnetic North. Using Parallel rules or a plotter you can work out the bearing of one object from another. This will tell you the compass course you should steer to get to one point from the other.

LIGHTHOUSES AND BUOYS

The seas near coasts have many hidden dangers. There may be rocks or reefs or sandbanks near shipping channels.

These dangers are usually marked by tall lighthouses or floating buoys. Lighthouses and buoys are fixed points which help sailors to navigate safely and find their positions.

Most of the big and important lighthouses are on headlands. Some, such as the Minot's Ledge near Boston, the Alligator Reef in Florida, and the Skerrymore in the British Isles are built on rocks in the water.

Nowadays most lights are remote controlled and have no full-time keepers.

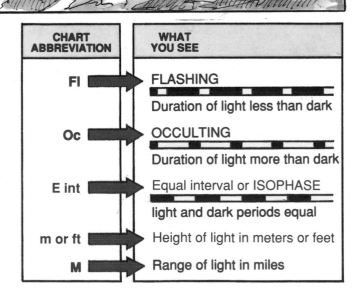

This lighthouse, the Skerrymore, ▶
was built in 1837-44 on the highest
point of a vicious reef to the south
of the Western Isles. On completion
it was the tallest, heaviest rock
tower ever built.

Characteristics of a Light

When you look at a lighthouse at night, you will see the light flashing. Did you realize that there is a pattern to the flashes? For instance the light may flash twice every ten seconds. This is called the light's *characteristic*. There are also *occulting* lights where the period of darkness is shorter than the period of light.

Sailors can identify lights by their characteristics. Each one has a different pattern of flashes from the lights nearby, so that when ships approach the coast, there is no chance of confusing one light with another. Charts also show the height of the light and the range at which it can be seen.

CHART ABBREVIATION	WHAT YOU SEE
Fl	FLASHING — Duration of light less than dark
Oc	OCCULTING — Duration of light more than dark
E int	Equal interval or ISOPHASE — light and dark periods equal
m or ft	Height of light in meters or feet
M	Range of light in miles

36

Buoys

Buoys are floating aids to navigation, They come in different shapes and colors, and some have lights. Their main function is to indicate the channels for entering and leaving harbors, and otherwise to warn of hidden dangers. The picture on the right shows the international system as it applies overseas. The picture below reflects the buoyage system for the Western Hemisphere, including the U.S. and Canada.

This channel buoy has ▶ a red light. The radar reflector on top makes it easier to detect on a ship's radar.

Most powerful lights are white because they can be seen from a greater distance. The light below is a small harbor warning light. It has a range of five miles.

▼

RED CAN BUOY

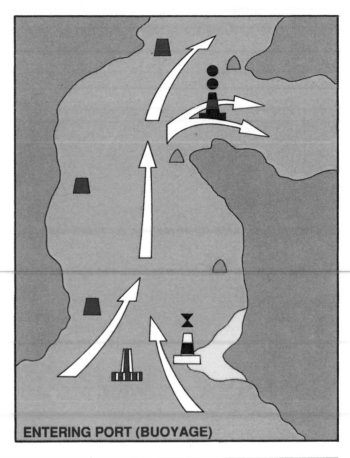

ENTERING PORT (BUOYAGE)

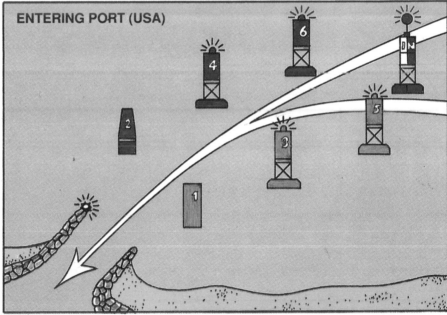

ENTERING PORT (USA)

▲
Important: Remember these simple rules for sailing in American waters. RED, RIGHT, RETURNING tells you the red buoys must be on your right when you are returning home. The reverse is just as easy to remember: RED, LEFT, LEAVING.

FLAGS

Ships have flown flags ever since they have had masts to put them on. The main purposes of flags were to identify the ship and to communicate with other vessels.

Radio telephones have now taken the place of flags for most forms of signalling. Even so merchant ships will still carry a full set of International Code flags. The flags she flies will tell you a lot about a ship.

Ensigns and Burgees

The ensign is usually flown at a ship's stern and shows to which country she belongs. The ensign may not be the same as the national flag.

Small craft such as dinghies do not usually fly flags, but most yachts will do so. If the owner of a yacht belongs to a sailing club, he will fly the club's own flag, a triangular flag called a burgee. Yachts do not fly an ensign when they are racing.

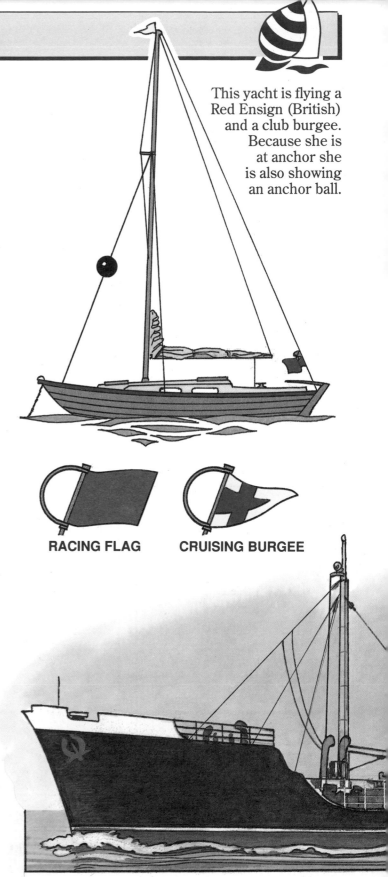

This yacht is flying a Red Ensign (British) and a club burgee. Because she is at anchor she is also showing an anchor ball.

RACING FLAG　　**CRUISING BURGEE**

FLAGS FLOWN AT SEA

UK (Ensign)	USA (Ensign)	FRANCE
GERMANY	HOLLAND	ITALY
NORWAY	SWEDEN	DENMARK

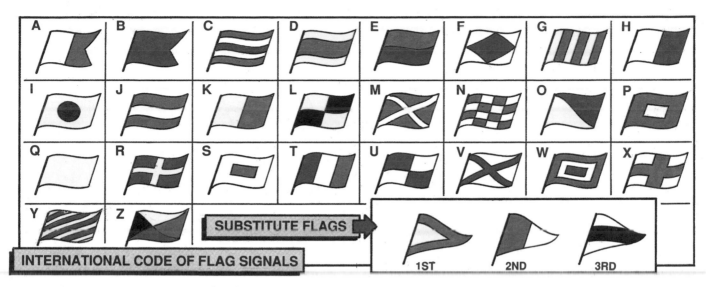

SUBSTITUTE FLAGS → 1ST 2ND 3RD

INTERNATIONAL CODE OF FLAG SIGNALS

This tanker comes from Rotterdam and so she is flying the Dutch Ensign at her stern. When vessels visit a foreign port, it is the custom to fly the ensign of the country being visited. This is called a Courtesy Flag. In this picture the courtesy flag is British.

At the masthead is the House Flag of the company which owns her. The red flag (international code flag B) shows that she is carrying fuel or explosives. The red and white flag (international code flag H) indicates that she is carrying a pilot.

▼

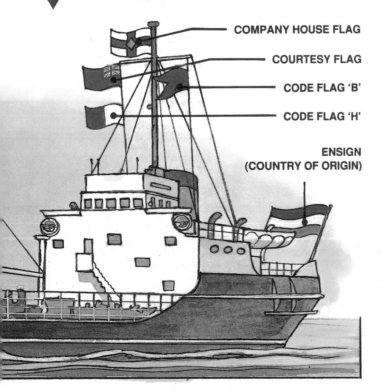

COMPANY HOUSE FLAG

COURTESY FLAG

CODE FLAG 'B'

CODE FLAG 'H'

ENSIGN (COUNTRY OF ORIGIN)

Identifying vessels
Merchant ships and yachts have their names painted on their stern. American yachts show the town and state:
    BAGATELLE
    Larchmont, NY
Some foreign boats show the initials of their club.

INT. CODE FLAG 'P'

The 'Blue Peter' (International code flag P) is flown by a vessel that is about to sail.

INT. CODE FLAG 'Q'

Flag Q. A vessel flying this flag has arrived from a foreign port and needs Customs clearance.

39

A PLACE FOR EVERYONE

The sea is big, but most people enjoy their water sports in their favorite coastal areas. Many different activities can take place in the same area at the same time – and they don't always fit together.

Almost any water sport can be dangerous to others. A swimmer may be injured by a sailboard. A windsurfer could be upset by a power boat. A water ski boat can cause a lot of damage in a collision. Everyone must use care and common sense.

Local Rules
Before you go afloat, ask if there are any local rules Ask a lifeguard, or someone at the local sailing club. In many places there are special areas allocated for various sports.
- If there is a special area for your sport, stay within it – but keep a look-out for others who may have strayed.
- If there is no special area, keep an even better look-out for other people.

◀ This windsurfer should not be in the swimmer's area. He should also have looked where he was going.

◀ The blue and white flag (international code flag A) shows that there are divers in the water nearby, and all craft should keep clear.

It may be fun to drive a boat fast. But it is also extremely stupid if it is disturbing others. Observe posted speed limits.
▼

The Rules of the Road

Just as there are traffic rules for driving a car, there is also a set of rules for the sea. They are known as the 'Rules of the Road'. The full list is long and complicated. As a young sailor you do not have to know it all, but there are a few simple rules that you should learn. Remember that these rules apply to windsurfers as much as they do to other sailors.

The rules also say that 'power gives way to sail'. But that does not mean that a sailboard should suddenly dash under the bows of a motor boat. Common sense is always needed.

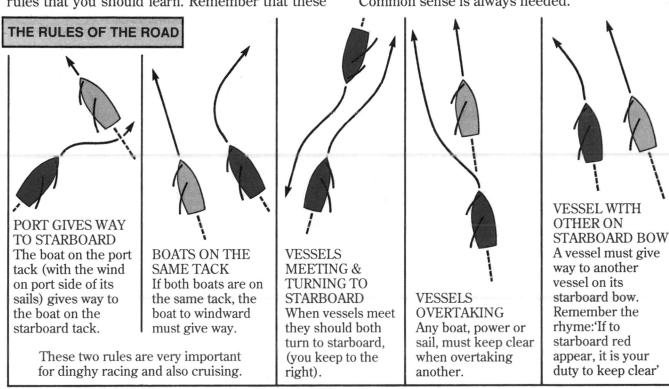

THE RULES OF THE ROAD

PORT GIVES WAY TO STARBOARD
The boat on the port tack (with the wind on port side of its sails) gives way to the boat on the starboard tack.

These two rules are very important for dinghy racing and also cruising.

BOATS ON THE SAME TACK
If both boats are on the same tack, the boat to windward must give way.

VESSELS MEETING & TURNING TO STARBOARD
When vessels meet they should both turn to starboard, (you keep to the right).

VESSELS OVERTAKING
Any boat, power or sail, must keep clear when overtaking another.

VESSEL WITH OTHER ON STARBOARD BOW
A vessel must give way to another vessel on its starboard bow. Remember the rhyme:'If to starboard red appear, it is your duty to keep clear'

Beware of Big Ships

Remember that a big merchant ship cannot stop suddenly and take avoiding action like a car. A large tanker may take at least two miles to stop. She can't alter course quickly either.

Big ships cannot steer into shallow water like a small boat or they will go aground. Sailors in small craft must keep their eyes open for bigger ships and keep out of their way.

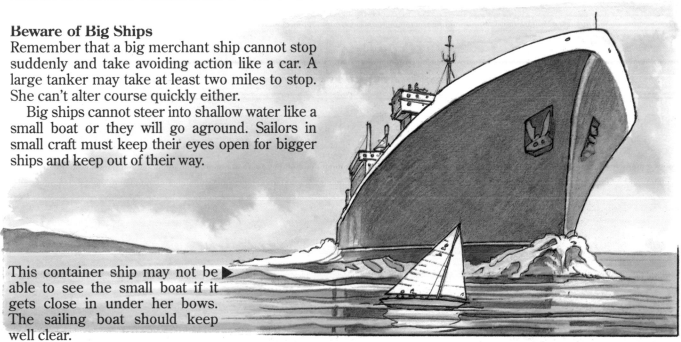

This container ship may not be able to see the small boat if it gets close in under her bows. The sailing boat should keep well clear.

PLAYING SAFE

Inexperienced sailors and windsurfers may look tough if they go out in high winds. But they don't look so tough when they have to be rescued. Sailing is fun. Don't spoil the fun by getting into trouble. Nobody can afford to ignore the basic safety rules, no matter how experienced they may be.

DO	DON'T
• Wear a lifejacket (PFD) if advised to, or if local rules say so. • Keep a good lookout for swimmers and other craft. • Tell someone where you are going and when you will get back.	• Go sailing unless you are properly dressed to keep warm. The wind feels colder when you are afloat. • Go out in a boat that is not properly equipped. (See page 17 and ask if in doubt.) • Forget to watch the weather – it can change suddenly.

▲ This is an experienced sailor. In rough weather he is wearing a lifejacket and a safety harness with a lanyard to prevent him getting lost overboard.

▲ This windsurfer has had to be rescued. He was not watching the weather, and the wind was too strong for him to get back to the beach.

QUIZ

1. What is this flag and what does it mean?

2. In a boat, what is the opposite of 'forward'?

3. What do you call the line used to hoist a sail?

4. What is the boom in a sailboard usually called?

5. On which side of the channel do you find this buoy when you are coming into a harbor?

6. In a small boat, what is a painter used for?

7. Where is the wind in relation to your boat when you are 'running'?

8. What is this boat fitting called?

9. What is an 'isobar'

10. What is the 'range' of the tide?

11. On the chart on page 33, name the other big lighthouse in addition to the Longships.

12. What is a 'sounding'?

13. What does this symbol on a chart mean, and why do you think they are shown on charts?

14. Is this a racing flag or a cruising burgee?

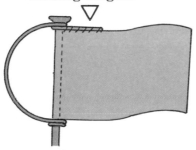

15. What would it mean if you saw a boat flying this flag?

16. What is a 'forestay'?

17. What is the binding at the end of a rope called?

18. On a compass how many degrees is due South?

19. What is this knot called and where do you use it?

20. In which direction should a rope be coiled?

Answers

1. Flag P (The Blue Peter). This flag means the ship is about to sail. **2.** Aft. **3.** Halyard. **4.** Wishbone. **5.** Starboard (or right hand) side. **6.** Rope used for tying up the boat at dock. **7.** Astern or behind you. **8.** Cleat. **9.** A line on a weather map joining places with the same barometric pressure. **10.** Difference between high water and low water (or high tide and low tide). **11.** Pendeen. **12.** Depth of water shown on chart. **13.** A church. Shown on a chart because tower or spire may be visible from the sea and useful for checking position. **14.** Racing flag. **15.** There are divers down nearby and you should keep well clear at low speed. **16.** The rigging from the masthead to the bow. **17.** A whipping. **18.** 180 degrees. **19.** Figure of eight knot. Used to prevent a rope slipping through a block. **20.** Clockwise.

43

GLOSSARY

You will have met several new words and expressions in this book. Here is a reminder of some of them, together with a few other words that are not in the book, but are useful to know.

Amidships: In the middle of a boat or ship.
Astern: Towards the stern or behind a boat.
Batten: A strip of wood or plastic used to keep a sail in shape.
Beam: The widest part of a boat's hull.
Bear away: To steer away from the direction of the wind.
Beat (to): To sail to windward.
Beaufort Scale: Scale used for expressing the strength of the wind.
Block: A pulley used afloat – there are many types and sizes.
Bowline: A type of knot that makes a loop.
Characteristic: The pattern of light flashes from a buoy or lighthouse.
Cleat: A fitting for securing the end of a rope.
Clew: The rear corner of a sail.
Coming about: See *tack*.
Compass rose: Compass depicted on a chart for working out courses and bearings.
Cordage: A ship's ropes and lines.
Draft: The depth of a vessel below the waterline.
Ease: To pay out or let out a rope.
Ebb (tide): The flow of the falling tide.
Ensign: A country's maritime flag.
Flood (tide): The flow of the rising tide.
Foot: The bottom edge of a sail.
Forestay: The rigging that supports the mast from forward.
Gooseneck: Fitting which secures the boom to the mast.
Gunwale: Top of the sides of a boat. (Pronounced *gunnal*)
Halyard: A line used for hoisting a sail.
Head: [1] The upper corner of a sail.
   [2] The toilet compartment on a vessel.
Heel: [1] The laying over of a boat to leeward.
   [2] The bottom of the mast.
Isobar: A line drawn on a weather map joining points with the same atmospheric pressure.
Jib: The triangular sail carried forward of the mast.
Jibe: To turn so that the wind crosses the stern.
Knot: (speed) One nautical mile per hour.
Leeward: Direction which is away from the wind.
Leech: The trailing edge of a sail.

Line: The correct term for a rope used on board a vessel.
Log: [1] A ship's 'diary' in which details of a voyage are written. [2] A device for measuring a boat's speed and distance travelled (taffrail log).
Lubber's line: The fixed line on a compass pointing forward to the bow.
Luff: The forward edge of a sail.
Luff up: To steer a boat up into the wind.
Neap tides: Tides with the smallest rise and fall. (See *range*)
Painter: A line used to secure a dinghy.
PFD: Personal Flotation Device, or lifejacket - worn by sailors for safety.
Point of sail: The direction of sailing in relation to the wind.
Range (of the tide): The difference between high water and low water.
Reach (to): To sail with the wind on the beam.
Reef (to): To reduce the sail area as the wind strength increases.
Run (to): To sail with the wind astern.
Shackle: A metal fitting for joining rigging or chain.
Sheet: The line used for controlling a sail.
Shipshape: Neat and tidy – as any boat should be.
Shoal: An area of shallow water.
Shroud: The rigging supporting the mast on either side.
Slack water: The period at high and low water when the tide hardly moves.
Sounding: The charted depth of water at a particular place.
Spring tide: Tides with the greatest rise and fall. (See *Neap tides*)
Tack: [1] To alter course so that the eye of the wind passes across the bow. [2] The bottom forward corner of a sail.
Thwart: A seat placed across a small boat.
Tidal current: The horizontal movement of the tide.
Topsides: The area of hull between the deck and the waterline.
Transom: The flat boards forming the stern of a boat.
Weather: The direction from which the wind is blowing – thus the *weather side*.
Whipping: Preventing a rope's end fraying by binding it with twine.
Windward: Towards the wind.